The Reminiscences of the

Honorable Colgate W. Darden, Jr.

U.S. Naval Institute

Annapolis, Maryland

1984

Preface

One of the earliest series of interviews undertaken by Dr. John T. Mason after he became the Naval Institute's director of oral history in 1969 focused on individuals who had served as U.S. naval aviators during World War I. One such individual whom he interviewed that first year was Colgate W. Darden, Jr., who won his wings in 1918 and then went to France as a Marine Corps flier in the closing months of the war. Marine aviation was then still in its infancy, as indicated by Darden's explanation that he wasn't able to do much flying because there were few planes available. His last flight wound up as a spectacular tragedy. While in the rear seat of a De Havilland DH-4 on 25 October 1918, less than three weeks before the end of the war, Darden was involved in a crash which injured him badly and killed the pilot, Medal of Honor winner Ralph Talbot.

In the years that followed, Darden went on to a distinguished career as a member of the U.S. House of Representatives, as Governor of Virginia, and as President of the University of Virginia. Because Dr. Mason's initial interview turned out to be so interesting, he went back to Governor Darden a few weeks later and got him to talk about his service on the House Naval Affairs Committee in the 1930s and early 1940s. This was the time of rearmament as the United States prepared to fight World War II. Darden explains the ways in which President Franklin D. Roosevelt worked with Congress to achieve his program, and he also covers the very strong and effective leadership that Chairman Carl Vinson exerted in running the Naval Affairs Committee.

Governor Darden had an opportunity to go over transcripts of these two oral interviews. His corrections and additions have been incorporated in the version which follows. Ms. Susan Sweeney has done a very capable job in editing the transcript and providing footnotes to explain further many of the things discussed by Darden. Deborah Reid of Techni-Type did the smooth typing of the transcript. Valuable assistance in the compilation of the brief biographical sketch was provided by Mrs. Colgate W. Darden, Jr., and Dr. C.W. Darden III.

                                                      Paul Stillwell
                                                      Director of Oral History
                                                      U.S. Naval Institute
                                                      August 1984

COLGATE WHITEHEAD DARDEN, JR.

Mr. Darden was born 11 February 1897 on a farm in Southampton County in the southern tidewater region of Virginia. He was the son of Colgate W. Darden and Katherine Pretlow Darden. His father was a banker.

Young Darden was educated in Virginia public schools and was graduated from high school in 1913. He enrolled in the University of Virginia at the age of 16 but left school to serve with the French Army as an ambulance driver during World War I. On 28 August 1917, he enlisted as a seaman second class in the U.S. Naval Reserve Force at Washington, D.C., and subsequently took flight training at the Massachusetts Institute of Technology and at naval air stations in Miami and Pensacola, Florida. He was commissioned as a second lieutenant in the Marine Corps Reserve on 17 July 1918 and sent overseas. He arrived in France on 31 July 1918 and was assigned to the Northern Bombing Group. On 25 October 1918, he was seriously injured in an aircraft accident which killed Second Lieutenant Ralph Talbot, USMCR, a Medal of Honor winner for his aviation exploits in World War I. Darden was retired in August 1919 because of his "...incapacity resulting from an incident of service with the temporary rank held on retirement," which was second lieutenant, U.S. Marine Corps Reserve.

After recovering from his injuries, Darden enrolled once again at the University of Virginia and was graduated in 1922 with a B.A. degree. He then earned his M.A. and LL.B. degrees from Columbia University and spent an additional year studying international law at Oxford University's Christ Church College on a Carnegie fellowship.

Mr. Darden's political career began in 1929 after he was elected to the Virginia House of Delegates from Norfolk. He served two two-year terms, then was elected in 1932 to the U.S. House of Representatives from Virginia's Second Congressional District. In 1936, having aroused President Franklin D. Roosevelt's displeasure because of his lukewarm support of the New Deal, Congressman Darden was defeated in the general election. He won his seat back in the 1938 election and was reelected in 1940. Throughout his time in Congress, Darden served as a member of the House Naval Affairs Committee. In the spring of 1941 he resigned from Congress in order to prepare to run for the governorship of Virginia; he won election in 1942 and served a four-year term. Among his achievements as governor were instituting civilian defense measures in Virginia during World War II, improving schools throughout the state, retiring the debt Virginia had carried since post-Civil War Reconstruction days, increasing wages for teachers and state employees, and paving the way for postwar construction at various state institutions.

In October 1946, even though offered a chance to go into the U.S. Senate to take the place of Carter Glass, who had died, Governor Darden chose instead to become chancellor of the College of William and Mary at Williamsburg, Virginia. He held that post until October 1947, when he was inaugurated as president of the University of Virginia at Charlottesville. He served as president for 12 years, until 1959. His tenure was noted for his achievements in shoring up the school's graduate program, improving faculty salaries, opposing the domination of social fraternities on campus, and overseeing the construction of $17 million worth of new buildings. He made the university into a more democratic institution than it had been, placing the emphasis on students' ability rather than their families' social standing. He served briefly as a U.S. delegate to the United Nations in 1955, during his tenure as university president.

During the 1950s, Governor Darden opposed the movement in Virginia aimed at staunch resistance to the racial integration of public schools. In the 1960s, he was instrumental in reopening schools which had been closed as a means of avoiding integration. In 1964, he was named first president-emeritus of the University of Virginia. The university's graduate school of business was named in his honor, as was the school of education at Old Dominion University in Norfolk. In the closing years of his life, Governor Darden was widely regarded as Virginia's elder statesman. He died on 9 June 1981 at his home in Norfolk.

Governor Darden's family included his wife, the former Constance S. du Pont; his son Colgate W. Darden III; another son, Pierre Darden, who was lost at sea at the age of 26 while sailing in the Atlantic in 1959; and a daughter, Mrs. Irene Darden Field.

A volume of oral history concerning Governor Darden's career as a whole is available, although it does not concentrate on the Navy and Marine Corps aspects to the extent that this Naval Institute version does. It is _Colgate Darden: Conversations with Guy Friddell_ (Charlottesville: University Press of Virginia, 1978).

Authorization

The U.S. Naval Institute is hereby authorized to make available to individuals, libraries, and other repositories of its choosing the transcripts (or portions thereof) of two oral history interviews concerning the career of the late Colgate W. Darden, Jr. The two interviews were tape-recorded by Mr. Darden, in collaboration with Dr. John T. Mason, Jr., of the Naval Institute on 24 September 1969 and 20 October 1969.

Acting on behalf of the estate of the late Mr. Darden, the undersigned does hereby release and assign to the U.S. Naval Institute all right, title, restrictions, and interest in the two interviews. The tape recordings of the interviews shall be the sole property of the Naval Institute. The copyright in both the oral and transcribed versions shall also be the sole property of the Naval Institute.

Signed and sealed this 10th day of August, 1984.

Constance S. du Pont Darden
(Mrs. Colgate W. Darden, Jr.)

Interview Number 1 with the Honorable Colgate W. Darden, Jr.

Place: Army and Navy Club, Washington, D.C.

Date: 24 September 1969

Subject: Naval Aviation

Interviewer: John T. Mason, Jr.

Q: Governor Darden, it is certainly pleasant indeed to meet you this morning. I am so grateful to you for your willingness to cooperate with the Naval Institute in this project on naval aviation, especially in the very early days. Governor, I know from the biographical sketch of your military service that way back in 1916 you had some service with the French Army. Would you tell me about that, Sir?

Mr. Darden: I did. There was tremendous enthusiasm at the University of Virginia where I was a student in 1916--I had entered there in the fall of 1914--in the Allied cause. I joined in the summer of 1916 three other boys and entered the French service. We went to Paris. There was Clark Lindsey, who was the publisher of The Daily Progress, who died a few months back, Douglas Bolling, and Bobbie Gooch.*
Bobbie has recently retired as a professor at the University of

---

*Clark E. Lindsey; Douglas T. Bolling; Robert R. Gooch. The Daily Progress is a daily newspaper published in Charlottesville, Virginia. The names of all the volunteers in the American Field Service and several personal narratives concerning their experiences can be found in Friends of France (Boston: Houghton Mifflin, 1916).

Virginia. We crossed the Atlantic in July of 1916 and shortly thereafter...

Q: Did you have any difficulty arranging transportation?

Mr. Darden: No, we crossed on the French Line on the old <u>Chicago</u>, and there was no difficulty. They provided for it. It was a gloomy trip, because it was a trip with all lights out at night. There was a good deal of speculation as to whether or not we would get intercepted by a German submarine. The ship was carrying not many passengers but a great deal of supplies for the French Army. We went into Bordeaux.

Q: You still were in your teens at that time.

Mr. Darden: Yes, I was. I was 19. We went on to Paris and after a few days---maybe a week or ten days there---we were shuffled off to the front. I went with Section One that was at Verdun. The French were then, and had been for some months, under terrific pressure from the German armies at Verdun, and there I served.*

Q: Your period of ten days in Paris was a period of indoctrination?

---

*From February to December 1916, the French repelled a large-scale German offensive in one of the major battles on the Western Front. The city of Verdun was nearly destroyed, and the loss of life totaled 750,000.

Mr. Darden: Yes, it was there at the headquarters. Piatt Andrew was the head of the American Field Service, and that's where I first came to know him.* I knew him quite well later.

Q: He was a Congressman, was he?**

Mr. Darden: He was a Congressman. Later he and I served in the House of Representatives together and I saw a good deal of him.

Q: I knew him, yes.

Mr. Darden: He was a very nice person. We had a period of indoctrination—a very short period, though. The need of the service was great. We moved on up, and I went up to Section One, which was then just back of the city of Verdun. We were taking out the wounded for the French from the lines beyond Verdun. The French, as you remember, had stopped the Germans in the general vicinity of Douaumont and Vaux. They had then, I think, lost both of those fortresses. But they had stopped them in the line along the hills beyond the city—beyond the river. The artillery fire there was awfully heavy, and the

---

*A. Piatt Andrew, Jr., Inspector General of the American Field Service with the Army of France from 1914 to 1917. The American Field Service was a group of American volunteers, mostly college students, who joined with French troops in various capacities during the two and a half years before the United States became officially involved in World War I.
**Andrew served as a Republican representative from Massachusetts from 1921 until his death in 1936.

roads were raked by German artillery by the day, so we drove at night. And the driving at night without lights was just unbelievable. It can be done and can be done better than you think really. But it takes some learning and takes some doing, more especially when you have to dodge, as we did, the heavy trucks carrying ammunition and troops that were moving up and down the road and moving as rapidly as they could, because the Germans kept the roads under fire at night also. They didn't do too much damage, but they slowed traffic tremendously, because nobody knew when they were going to zip in---or zero in, as the expression is now---on a particular part of the road. I served there until the winter when we were moved down for the great Champagne offensive that the French were planning and which was disastrous. Their losses down there were simply horrible. And we were stopped---we didn't get down to our final destination. We were stopped at Bois de la Grange and stayed there until spring when I was sent to the hospital because of a bronchial infection.

Q: May I interrupt with a question? Your transition from student life at the University of Virginia to the battlefront in France was so very sudden and the time so very short. Did this present any problems for you young fellows, emotionally speaking?

Mr. Darden: No, it didn't. And you're quite right. It was a transition from serenity and peace to complete war; the death and destruction at Verdun were just beyond description. But there was

Darden #1 - 5

enormous enthusiasm among those of us who were serving there with the French, and that buoyed us up. And I think we were buoyed up further by the fact that we didn't know what a dangerous undertaking we were engaged in. As I look back on it now, I shiver. But then it seemed part and parcel of a new world---another world---and then there was underlying all our endeavors the belief that later on was found in the American Expeditionary Force---a firm belief that we were building a new world, we were laying the foundation for a society in which war would disappear.

Q: And your idealism carried you through there.

Mr. Darden: It carried you right along through. And it was true of all of us. I knew a number of those boys that were over there, and they all felt the same way about it. They were glad to be part and parcel of it. They were frightened. All of us were frightened, because we had never been under shellfire in our lives, and we were not prepared for the wreckage of vehicles and things of that kind that we saw. Nor were we prepared for the death that we saw and then the death of the severely wounded that we were trying to get out of the lines, who sometimes died before we could get them to the hospital. It was a grim experience, really. But it did not destroy our enthusiasm---at least I didn't sense it at the time.

Q: One further question: did your family share in this idealism which

Darden #1 - 6

you had?

Mr. Darden: They did to a degree. I think they were very apprehensive about my going, but they saw how much I wanted to go and gave over to it. But I'm sure that it must have meant some long, painful days for my mother and father—both of them were living then—and my brother and sister. There were five of us.

Q: That was a tangent that I got off on.

Mr. Darden: After I was taken out for bronchial trouble—I had a very severe, a very difficult time—the French sent me down on the Riviera finally in an effort to see if sunshine would help me along. And it did. It was slow; it was a serious congestion. Then, in a little while, we were in the war, so I came on back to the United States and signed up in naval aviation.

Q: Why did you do that, Sir?

Mr. Darden: I don't know just why, except that, of course, all Tidewater Virginia is committed to the Navy. It's a naval area, and while I did not live in Norfolk then—I lived close by in Southampton County, which was only 50 miles from Norfolk—we were intimately related and had been through history to Hampton Roads and the goings-on there. I think that had much to do with it really,

Darden #1 - 7

unconsciously, that I was affected.

Q: It was a natural affinity you had for it.

Mr. Darden: Yes. And then of course the Navy had a small naval aviation station in Hampton Roads, and there was a good deal in the paper about it.

Q: Had you ever visited there?

Mr. Darden: I did visit there when I was trying to get in the Navy. It was just across the roads in Newport News, and the planes were flying around Hampton Roads. Of course, planes were a novelty then. They were not what they are now; they were rare. That was in the spring of '17. There was a delay in calling us up. There were many of us in naval aviation waiting to be called up. It wasn't until early fall that I went to Tech and started in the ground school. As I remember it, it was about the first of October. I think the ground school course was three or four months.

Q: Where was that?

Mr. Darden: Massachusetts Institute of Technology. They sent us there for ground school work.

Darden #1 - 8

Q: Can you say something about the training course?

Mr. Darden: It was very good. They put us through a good deal of drilling, and they emphasized discipline. They had courses in mathematics and things of that kind that were good and not too difficult for those of us who had had good college mathematics.

Q: What was your college status?

Mr. Darden: I was two years there in the College of Arts and Sciences at the University of Virginia when I left for the French service. I did not go back until after the war. I did not go back to college after my French service. I came back and started on the naval aviation, signed up for naval aviation. We had a long course in semaphoring, which none of us ever mastered, although we put on a lot of airs about being able to semaphore. We were absolutely hopeless in it. We couldn't do a thing in the world with it, but the Navy just shoved us along. They were under great pressure to get us along through and to get us out to a training school.

Q: How large a class of recruits was there?

Mr. Darden: I was in Company 9, and, as I remember it, there must have been 30 or 35 of them or something of that order. We were let out for Christmas. I'll never forget that. They permitted us to go

Darden #1 - 9

for Christmas which was a bonus that none of us had expected. We came back in January and then were graduated in January and sent off---we were broken up and sent off to flying stations. A small group of us, the little group that I was with, were sent to Miami. We left just around the first of February. I remember the contrast of the sunshine and the warmth of Miami, which was then a little country town---it wasn't anything like the great metropolitan area it is now---and the snow we left in Boston was deep and cold. And for those of us who had come out of warmer climates, it was terribly cold. We just weren't prepared for anything like that. It was a great relief to us to get down to Miami. Marc Mitscher was commanding there.[*] He was then a young commander.

Q: What kind of installations did they have there?

Mr. Darden: They had a good naval station, the old Coral Gables station down in Coral Gables. It's all gone now. But the Navy apparently changed its mind about training us after they got us to Miami. We stayed there only a few days. Then we were picked up and sent to Pensacola, which was a very much more ambitious station, although very primitive. The number of students was very much greater, as was the number of planes.

---

[*]Lieutenant Commander Marc A. Mitscher, USN, commanding officer of Naval Air Station Miami in 1918-1919. Mitscher was a noted carrier admiral in World War II.

Darden #1 - 10

Q: How long had Pensacola been in operation at that time?

Mr. Darden: Well, Pensacola, of course, is a very old naval station. But it had been, I think, a few years in naval aviation training, and for a few months prior to our arrival it had been receiving recruits in some numbers.

Q: For flying.

Mr. Darden: Yes. We were there, and it was there that we went through flying school.

Q: Tell me something about the vicissitudes of that.

Mr. Darden: It was tremendously interesting. I went back, interestingly enough, when I was in the House of Representatives, to Pensacola. I was on the Naval Affairs Committee then, and I went with a group on one occasion down there to inspect it and see how things were going on. I had heard a lot about what had been done at Pensacola, but I was not prepared for the enormous growth and the great modern steel hangars and concrete runways and things of that kind. We had large tents as hangars. We had stowed our planes in them. We'd fly during the day. We'd fly a good deal during the day. They got us up about daylight, and they would march us over to the mess hall where they'd give us a pretty ample-looking breakfast. But

I will never forget—it was my first introduction to powdered eggs. I think the Navy probably now has powdered eggs and waffles that are very good, but I never encountered a concoction that equaled the powdered eggs that we had in 1918. I'm sure they were healthy and good, because none of us ever got sick, but they were terrible things to eat. They'd dish them out to us, and it was eat or starve. So we ate.

We marched everywhere. We never moved around on our own. The Navy had us in formation and marching us around. We were all rookies, and as I remember, none of us had ever had any military training. In my experience with the French, I had never been given any marching or discipline of that kind. We'd go down, and then we'd fly all day long except when we marched back for lunch and back to the beach. We had good instructors. They were nice people. I think some of them were civilians employed by the Navy to instruct us. Some were naval officers but very few. The Navy did not have many naval aviators then—just a handful of them.

Q: What planes did you use?

Mr. Darden: We used, as I remember, the old N-9, which was a single-pontoon plane—I think I'm right.* And then later on for more

---

*The Curtiss N-9, which had a maximum speed of 80 miles per hour, was the Navy's standard primary and advanced seaplane trainer of World War I. It had a heavy central float and two small stabilizing floats at the ends of the lower wing.

Darden #1 - 12

advanced flying, we had a double-pontoon. I think it was called the R-6.* The N-9 was a very reliable plane. It was quite safe. If it stalled, it would not stall into a spin as so often happens with, or did back in those days, in training planes. It would simply stall, poke its nose up in the air, and settle down until it gained enough flying speed to go along again.

Q: Did you have any training with gliders?

Mr. Darden: No, we had no training with gliders, because they had no gliders there that I have any recollection of. We'd shut off for supper about 5:00 o'clock, and then we'd march up. Then we'd be marched back down to the hangars to wash off the planes. The salt water was very damaging to the fittings, and it had to be gotten off the plane or the rust would give them difficulty. Then the dope used on the wings—the finishing used on the wings was a type of varnish that we called dope—had to be washed down; otherwise the salt would peel that off. So every night we spent an hour or a couple of hours washing planes, which was part and parcel of our service, and nobody objected to it. Everybody was ready and willing to do it. Then we'd be carried back to our barracks, and we'd turn in about 9:00 or 10:00 o'clock. We slept in a long loft that the Navy had turned over for our group. We slept up there. The cots were not too close together,

---

*The Curtiss R-6, with a maximum speed of 100 miles per hour, did indeed have two pontoon floats on the undercarriage, as Darden remembered.

Darden #1 - 13

but they were lined up on each side of the loft.

Q: Did you have any classroom lectures or training of that sort?

Mr. Darden: I don't remember any classroom lectures at all at Pensacola.

Q: It was all action.

Mr. Darden: All action. I don't remember that we were ever called in and given a lecture of any kind.

Q: How many men were accommodated in a single N-9?

Mr. Darden: It carried two—in line in a narrow fuselage. They did the instructing in that, you see. The pupil would sit forward, and the instructor would sit behind him. We learned to fly in that way. The R-6 was two-passenger—in my recollection, the same way. It was a much larger plane, because it had two pontoons, and it had to have more wingspread to carry them.

Q: How long a period before you were given control of a plane?

Mr. Darden: My memory is that it took between nine and 12 hours of instruction before a student was turned loose. And then it took, of

Darden #1 - 14

course, no end of hour on hour flying around and acquainting yourself with it and practicing gunnery.

Q: Was this as solo?

Mr. Darden: Yes, as solo. Between nine and 12 hours they turned everybody that I knew loose on soloing.

Q: Were there any casualties?

Mr. Darden: A few casualties, but not many. There were a few boys lost in the landings. Landing on glassy water on a very quiet day is a right tricky operation. You misjudge the water. If there's a little wind blowing and if there are ripples or any activity, it's much easier to set the distances. But sometimes on the bay there at Santa Rosa Island, the bay between Santa Rosa Island and the mainland, it would be very still and very calm---it would be glass-like. There were a few accidents, but there were remarkably few really in the training thing. We were very fortunate in that way. The Navy was very careful in the training. The pressed us along and pushed us along, but they had good instructors, and they were very patient instructors and capable fellows. They went over and over the important things with us.

Q: Were there any in your group who simply weren't passed?

Darden #1 - 15

Mr. Darden: Yes, there were one or two who were thought not to have aptitude for flying, and it was suggested that they move on into some other work in aviation but not many. Most of us qualified as pilots. I think that was due to the fact that the physical examinations leading up to ground school and all had been quite thorough. And also the examinations when we got to Pensacola had weeded us out.

Q: They actually got eliminated along the way.

Mr. Darden: Yes.

Q: As a qualified pilot, were you also in a sense a qualified mechanic?

Mr. Darden: Yes, we were really. We did a great deal of work on planes helping the mechanics they had there. There were many of us who knew something about automobile engines. They were not unalike--- they were very much the same. We fell in and helped in anything that we could. There wasn't any line drawn so that one man was supposed to do one job and one man do another. They hadn't refined it to that point. I'm sure they have that now. They must have it for the vast operation that they have now. But in those days we moved from one occupation to another with a great deal of ease and a great deal of rapidity.

Darden #1 - 16

Q: What was the intended destination, intended use of these naval aviators?

Mr. Darden: I'm not sure about that, because I left and went over to the Marine Corps along with some fellows. The Marines wanted land pilots, but I think that the Navy was training them for missions along the coast and harbors in Europe and for operation with the fleet. But I never knew, because I had left the Navy by that time. In the spring of '18 a very interesting thing happened. Major Cunningham of the Marine Corps came into Pensacola and called together a certain number of us and explained that the Marines were attempting to equip several squadrons of land planes that they wanted to use inland with Marines that were in France.* They did not want to undertake to set up their own school and attempt to train them, because they didn't have time. They had made arrangements with the Navy---or rather the Navy I expect told them to do it, because the Marines are a part of the Navy---to get transfers for any of us that wanted to be transferred and fly land planes. They would then send us to their gunnery school and advanced plane school that was outside of Miami, not far from the station that we had first gone to.

Q: Not far from Coral Gables.

---

*Major Alfred A. Cunningham, USMC, Naval Aviator #5 and first U.S. Marine to train in aviation.

Darden #1 - 17

Mr. Darden: Not far from Coral Gables back inland. There's a little mark on the field now. A fair number of us decided that we would transfer to land planes. We had not been commissioned then. We were non-ensigns, but we were naval aviators. We had passed our tests. They were fairly simple tests. You had to go up to certain heights, cut our motor, and come down and land within a certain distance of a buoy; that wasn't so hard to do. And then run two or three other courses. We were all naval aviators but not commissioned. There was a great difficulty for us to get commissions, because Washington was piled up with work and we hadn't gotten our commissions. He said that didn't make any difference; he'd take us on over to Miami and commission us in the Marine Corps.

Q: And that was the real incentive for making this transfer?

Mr. Darden: One was a very small thing, but it had a powerful influence. In the spring of '18, the Navy introduced what they thought was their last word in a flying boat, the H-16, with two giant motors that stuck up behind the pilots in the struts.* The pilot was sitting out in the forward cockpit flying. It was a gigantic thing, and when we looked at that, we figured two things. One, that it would be cumbersome and difficult to fly; two, that in any accident there wouldn't be anybody left living, because those engines would slide

---

*The Curtiss H-16 had a gross weight of 10,900 pounds, compared with 2,765 pounds for the N-9 and 4,500 pounds for the R-6.

Darden #1 - 18

right forward and kill anyone sitting there in front of them. Which proved to be generally the case with such few accidents as they had. Fortunately, they didn't have too many.

Q: They didn't have parachutes then?

Mr. Darden: No, nobody had a parachute. Nobody ever dreamed of parachutes then. The H-16 was just too cumbersome. They were huge things. The Navy was very proud of them, but when you looked at them as something to fly, it cooled down most of us who were going to have to do the flying. So we decided that we would depart for smaller and more manageable and faster planes, and that, I think, had something to do with it. I know it had something to do with it--it had a good deal, because we talked amongst ourselves about it. We would never divulge that to the Marine Corps, nor did we ever mention that to the Navy, but it was a very compelling argument as we sat around in the night talking amongst ourselves or got together in little clusters around the beach to discuss what we were going to do. We had to move very quickly.

The next thing was that the Marine Corps gave us absolute assurance that they would send us at once to France, and the Navy still was undecided as to how they were going to use this new arm of the service, and that interested us and led us on to join up with the Marines.

Darden #1 - 19

Q: Because your idealism was still driving you on.

Mr. Darden: Yes. So we moved over and then moved down to Miami and to the Marine school there.

Q: What were the planes there? The land planes?

Mr. Darden: They were JN-4s, as I remember, with Hispano-Suiza motors.* It was a 180-horsepower motor, and it was a beautiful motor. All wooden propellers. All planes in those days had wooden propellers. They were very good planes. And then we had a Thomas Scout there that had a rotary motor, or it might have been a radial, but I think it was a rotary motor. It had a curious way that as it reached a certain speed its tail would wiggle vigorously, and that scared us to death, because we felt that it was only a question of time before the tail would wiggle off. It never did. No one that I knew of---I never knew of an accident with the Thomas Scout, but when you put it in a little dive, you just had to be prepared for the wiggling at your back that was quite disturbing. The JN is the one that we used, the JN-4 land biplane that we used in our advanced flying there. It was a graduate school and a gunnery school and all of that. We had some gunnery before we left the Navy. Highly

---

*According to Gordon Swanborough and Peter M. Bowers in United States Navy Aircraft Since 1911 (Annapolis: Naval Institute Press, 1976), page 102, the Curtiss JN-4H was equipped with a 150-horsepower Wright-Hispano engine.

inaccurate. We used to go and fire at a target and also practice a little in dropping bombs, none of which ever came in hailing distance of the target that I remember.

Q: You had no Norden bombsight or anything of the sort.*

Mr. Darden: No bombsight in them. I saw a very interesting thing happen on Santa Rosa Island one day. We were over, and we had had a break for lunch. We carried our lunches with us and took the break for lunch. During the lunch period, we'd usually go up and sweep off the target and, if need be, paint it. This day a couple of fellows—I was not included, I was watching from a distance—were sweeping off the target when, lo and behold, down the gunnery range came a plane. It was one of the planes that we had failed to take into account. We thought we had them all down. These fellows were coming right down on the target. The painters were down there scraping it, and the pilots opened up with their machine guns and ran right over the target, didn't touch a soul. Never touched a soul, just scared the hell out of them.

Q: You were grateful they weren't very accurate.

---

*The Norden bombsight was an optical device developed in the 1930s by Carl L. Norden, a civilian consultant to the Navy. It greatly improved the accuracy of bombing operations by keeping the plane level and straight during bomb runs.

Darden #1 - 21

Mr. Darden: I was very grateful that day, because they would have knocked those fellows right out. They were lying right down there on target and cleaning it up. At any rate, we went back to Miami, where we joined up with the Marines. We did a good deal of training at the land field there.

Q: How would you contrast the Marine instructors with the Navy instructors at Pensacola?

Mr. Darden: They were both good, and both services used a fair number of civilian instructors, civilian fliers that were brought in to help us. They were quite good. The Marines had more of their own officers flying with us. But there again, they had had a little more time to train, you see, because we went to Miami in the early summer or late spring of '18, and we went in the winter to Pensacola. Things were moving along rapidly in those days, so that even a few months made quite a difference in the number of pilots available to train. We were picked up in the late summer of 1918 and sent abroad with the Northern Bombing Group. I was in the First Squadron. The Marines had four squadrons that they had trained. Some pilots trained later went to the Azores. I'm not sure. I don't have any independent recollection as to how or where they were trained. I know the Marines had some pilots in the Azores.

Q: For what purpose would they be on the Azores?

Darden #1 - 22

Mr. Darden: They were submarine scouting and operating with the fleet.

Q: They again were flying pontoon planes.

Mr. Darden: I expect they were either pontoon or flying boats. I don't think they would in those days risk land planes over the water. It was thought to be very dangerous. We never went out over water in Florida in our training, although we were very close to water. We'd fly out to the coastline in a minute or so, but we never went out over the Atlantic with land planes to speak of.

Q: Did you practice with live bombs down there?

Mr. Darden: No, we never practiced with live bombs. We did do a great deal of practice with photograph-equipped machine guns in combat with each other. The development of that film would show about how accurate the firing was. It was a very ingenious thing. I'm sure it has been developed now to a point of perfection really for training pilots. Then, of course, the planes are so very fast now that the training is much more exacting. Our planes at best were slow, not much over 100 miles an hour.

Q: I see. As fighter planes they were 100...

Mr. Darden: Yes, the De Havilland that we had finally when we went abroad I think had a rated speed of 140 miles an hour with a Liberty motor.* I would doubt that it was that fast. I'd put 140 as tops for it. But we did no end of gunnery and training. But there again we didn't do much live machine gun training over there, as I remember. We did some, but very little of it. Now we had tried out with live machine guns in Pensacola over Santa Rosa Island, as I have mentioned.

Q: And there is a difference, isn't there?

Mr. Darden: Oh, there's a vast difference, yes, a good deal of difference.

Q: For somebody who is going into combat.

Mr. Darden: Yes, there's a vast difference. Well, one of the very great differences is that you get a vibration from a firing gun that's sizeable, a rapidly firing gun. You don't get one from a photography gun, a gun equipped with an aerial camera. You simply press the trigger and it clicks away, but there's no repercussion from that. We were not well-equipped, but we were as well-equipped as they could equip us, I think, at the time, and we knew little of the war. Even though it had been raging in Europe for some time, the amount of information that our armed forces had was limited.

---

*De Havilland DH-4 "Liberty Plane." Swanborough and Bowers credit it with a top speed of 122.5 miles per hour.

Darden #1 - 24

Q: And so then your training was completed and they shipped you abroad.

Mr. Darden: They shipped us abroad---I was just trying to think. They shipped us abroad in late summer of '18.

Q: How large a contingent of men?

Mr. Darden: I think four squadrons went abroad at one time. We were designated the Northern Bombing Group---day bombers---De Havillands, which were fighter-bombers. They called them fighter-bombers in those days, because they were unescorted and were supposed to be able to fend off attacks and to attack themselves, and several of the pilots did shoot down planes in combat. We did very little bombing, almost no bombing, because neither planes nor bombs were available. The marshalling of equipment was difficult in France, and we waited after we got there a long time before we got planes. The war was moving on toward the end before there were planes available.

Q: In ordnance, was that U.S. equipment?

Mr. Darden: Yes. We had our field between Calais and Dunkerque up near the coast. We were up with the British. Some of our people---I never did this---but some of our people flew with the British, went over with British squadrons and flew with them.

Darden #1 - 25

Q: Was that an optional thing?

Mr. Darden: I think it was optional, but it might have been arranged by the commander---Major Geiger commanded us and later commanded in the Pacific---of whom you know, I am sure.*

Q: Oh, yes.

Mr. Darden: Roy Geiger. He was our commanding officer. I think Cunningham was the overlord. I mean he was the Northern Bombing Group commander. I'm talking now about our first squadron. Geiger was our leader. I think maybe he might have arranged it and told these fellows to go over there and fly a bit. He might have arranged it at their request; I don't know. And I don't know that I ever did know that. But our part in the war was not great. We never were fully equipped. It was a small performance except in individual cases, a few individual pilots who were in combat.

Q: You must have gotten impatient then.

Mr. Darden: We did, we did. But it was an impatience that was understood. It was a failure to bring together the equipment and the pilots and the planes. But there again, we understood what a gigantic

---
*Major Roy S. Geiger, USMC. As a major general during World War II Geiger was director of Marine aviation (1943), the first aviator to command an amphibious corps (I Corps, Bougainville, 1943), and the first Marine to command an army (Tenth Army, Okinawa, June 1945).

Darden #1 - 26

effort this thing was and what a fearful undertaking it was. And for that reason, it wasn't an unpleasant unrest. There was never any real moodiness or sulkiness in the squadrons. We were in tents then, sitting out in a farm field in the French rains in the fall and the mud inches deep.

Q: That unrest was reserved for a future generation.

Mr. Darden: Yes, for another generation, who I really think at times don't understand what has gone on before them. But we had a tough top sergeant. Geiger turned us over to a top sergeant who ran us. Geiger was a good commander, but he didn't concern himself with us; he let this fellow run us. And he didn't like us really, because he was an old line Marine and we were reserves, and he didn't think that we were any good soldiers or much good anywhere. He was against us in principle, and he figured out ways to make life a little tough for us to give us an understanding that we were no longer back in college, but we were in the Marine Corps and that he was a Marine. So he worked up a plan of getting us up at daylight for formation. We didn't have a thing in the world to do---nothing. He would get us out to answer the roll at daylight, and if it was misty rain, so much the better. And in order to see that nobody could say that they slept through it, he assembled two or three buglers and would have them march down in front of the tents---we had a row of tents, one on each side of a little central street---not long, I think about maybe a hundred yards was the length of our company street---and these buglers

Darden #1 - 27

would march down one side and up the other bugling at the very top of their bugles. It would waken the dead. Nobody could sleep with that. Then he would get us up and line us up and make us line up properly, and then he would have a roll call. And that went on day after day. He would never let up on us. He never let up on us until we got out and the war was over. He bossed us around.

Q: How did he keep you occupied during the day?

Mr. Darden: He turned us loose to do more or less what we pleased. We used to kick football a great deal and play games of one kind and another.

Q: You didn't even practice gunnery.

Mr. Darden: No, we didn't have any planes, and we didn't practice on the ground. We couldn't practice on the ground. We were in a fairly well-populated area, in a farm area.

Q: So you might have seen greater service if you had stayed with the Navy.

Mr. Darden: We might have, although I think probably the early naval pilots had filled the berths—the limited number that they had abroad in the ports. So I don't know that we would have seen any more service than that.

Darden #1 - 28

Q: What was the status of the German Air Force, your adversary?

Mr. Darden: Oh, they were very good. They were apparently well-equipped. They used to come down and bomb us at night. Not bomb us, they never bombed us really. They'd fly over us going down to Calais to bomb Calais.

Q: They bombed at night?

Mr. Darden: Oh yes, they bombed a great deal at night.

Q: Were they accurate?

Mr. Darden: Fairly accurate. They had a curious motor that had a rhythm of rise and fall. It was unlike motors that we had. We could tell when they were coming way off. They had this hum of the motor that would grow in intensity and then drop away quickly. And we could tell they were coming. We'd know they were coming before they left their lines, because we weren't so far from their lines. They'd come down, and the only time they gave us any trouble, I think, was maybe dropping some bombs that they hadn't been able to get clear down at Calais, dropping near us on their way back home. But I don't believe and I don't know of anybody else that would believe they were trying to hit us.

Q: Do you think they were cognizant of your presence?

Darden #1 - 29

Mr. Darden: I doubt it. The tents were hard to make out at night. They were khaki tents flat down on the ground, and I don't believe they could see us. We couldn't see them. We could hear the motors. They weren't very high, but we couldn't see them.

Q: Was there any French force in existence to combat them?

Mr. Darden: No. There was no French force over in our part at least and no British force. Now antiaircraft would attempt to work on them, but that was extraordinarily inaccurate and never bothered them much. They'd go down usually about 9:00 or 10:00 o'clock and unload their bombs and turn around and go home.

Q: It was just a routine mission then.

Mr. Darden: Routine mission, yes.

Q: Were you on a zeppelin route?

Mr. Darden: No, I never saw a zeppelin. They were using them, of course.

Q: Yes, over in London.

Mr. Darden: But I never saw them in that part of the channel.

Darden #1 - 30

Q: You said that ultimately you did get equipment there.

Mr. Darden: We got equipment just toward the end of the war, and it was then that I was injured. So I was swept out and left.

Q: Tell me about your injury.

Mr. Darden: I was over at Squadron Three with a friend of mine, Ralph Talbot, and I went for a flight.* Talbot had been in a fight a day or two before, a few days before, and he had gotten his plane shot up right badly.** He had had it in the shop and had gotten it out. He and I had been in nine together. We were friends, and he had asked me to come along and go for a flight with him. I got in the plane and got in the gunner's seat. It was a DH-4. And for some reason I didn't fasten my belt. I just sat down on the gunner's seat on the strap that the gunner used as a seat in the mount that revolved and carried the machine gun. The gun wasn't mounted. We ran down the field, and there was trouble with the motor. I realized there was trouble. It wasn't tuned up well. Ralph came back, and then the second time he went down he got the plane about six inches off the ground and ran straight into a heap of earth that had been thrown up for a bomb pit at the end of this field. I think he must have known

---

*Second Lieutenant Ralph Talbot, USMCR.
**On 14 October 1918, eleven days prior to his flight with Darden, Talbot earned the Medal of Honor for his exceptional performance on a raid over Belgium. He was one of only two Marine Corps aviators awarded the Medal of Honor for World War I. The USS Ralph Talbot (DD-390) was named for him.

it but had forgotten about it. It was a bomb storage pit, dug at the end of the field, with earth thrown on the side as they dug this trench or hole. The DH locked its landing gear in the earth bank, and the plane went over into the pit. Talbot was killed, but I was thrown clear almost as though I had been thrown from a catapult. I was sitting in the second seat in the DH-4 and when she went over on her nose and turned over, she caught fire. It projected me straight out, just like a stone being thrown out of a catapult. It threw me 125 feet into a wheat field. Well, it was an awful fire, and the squadron boys ran down there to try to get us out and also to try to pull the bombs out of the way, because they didn't want them catching fire and exploding. They thought we both had been killed. They didn't see me take off on my flight, because the plane and the smoke interfered. I had been shot out at almost a dead level. I didn't go up and come down.

Q: You were like a missile.

Mr. Darden: I was just like a missile shooting at shoulder level, and it just shot me down on the ground. Walking around the field later on, they came across me and picked me up and put me in a car and took me over to the British hospital at Calais. There I stayed for a week or ten days or so. It was the end of October, the 25th, that I was injured. I was transferred from Calais to London.

Q: You had broken bones?

Darden #1 - 32

Mr. Darden: I had the right side of my face broken in completely. My head went over and hit the escarpment of the gun, and it crushed the side of my face. It dislocated my spine, the upper part of the spine, and paralyzed me. So it was some time before I could move. I was turned over by attendants at the hospital. They kept me on the bed and moved me around. Then, on my left leg, the flesh was just opened down to the bone, I think. My leg must have hit some blunt object. It didn't break the bone but simply pressed aside the flesh and opened it along the bone for two or three inches.

Q: It certainly was providential that you didn't fasten your flying belt.

Mr. Darden: Absolutely saved my life. Had I fastened that flying belt, I would have been burned. There was no way they could have gotten me out and I would have been...

Q: Did Talbot burn?

Mr. Darden: Talbot did, but I think he was killed immediately, because in the DH-4, one of its difficulties was that its large fuel tank of 90 gallons in a wreck would slide forward on the pilot. He was sitting in the pilot's seat, in the forward seat, which was the pilot's seat. I was sitting in the gunner's seat right behind the wings. It was a biplane. There was a 12- or 14-gallon auxiliary tank in the wing just above the pilot's head, and in a crash that thing

Darden #1 - 33

would come down and they would have a fire. That's what burned the plane up, and the 90-gallon tank tore out and went along with me for a distance, not as far. But the auxiliary tank caught fire on the impact. I think Talbot was killed instantly by the large tank moving forward and tearing out of the plane, because we hit with enormous force. We were off the ground, and I expect we were going 100 or 115 miles an hour and gaining headway. We were a little bit off the ground when we hit.

Q: Did they succeed in putting out the fire before the bombs exploded?

Mr. Darden: They got the bombs away from the fire. They got the bombs pulled away and there were no explosions.

Q: Tell me a little about the airfields of that day.

Mr. Darden: The airfields were simply graded fields, farming fields. There was no surfacing on them to speak of.

Q: No surfacing, no concrete or anything?

Mr. Darden: The most unbelievable field that I have ever seen or heard of was the field that we trained on in Miami. The dust there, the sand was six or eight inches deep. The planes would struggle terribly in taking off. You would open them full throttle, and they would struggle mightily at just a few miles an hour until they could extricate themselves and get up to the top of the sand and then coast along to take off. I don't know if you are a duck shooter. If you notice how a duck flies out of water, they run along a little way, gain headway, and then get up. Well, these planes would labor terribly and go slowly until they could finally pull themselves out and get away.

Q: Did that necessitate a very long runway?

Mr. Darden: Fairly long, yes. They were not like the runways are today, because the planes lifted off much more quickly. But the runways in France, the runways that we had were very imperfect. But then again, the planes weren't terribly heavy. The runways could be graded and fixed out.

Q: But this meant that in bad weather, the runways...

Mr. Darden: You were practically out of commission then.

Q: They used concrete as paving in those days.

Mr. Darden: I would expect that in the larger fields they had concrete runways fixed up. I think with us they probably had just some surfacing material that hardened the earth somewhat. But there again we had so few planes, and the war ended before we were equipped.

Darden #1 - 35

It ended before the field could be put in shape really for use.

Q: So this really was the end of your...

Mr. Darden: This was the end of my war career. I don't reckon anybody ever made a more modest contribution to the First World War than I made. But I went along, and I saw a lot, and I served with a lot of people who were good and interesting people and many of whom I have kept up with over the years. Many of them are dead now. It's startling how many are dead. We had our 50th reunion a year ago next month in Miami. We left there in 1918. We went back in 1968 for the 50th reunion and sat around and talked and lived over the old days. But there were not too many. A good many of them are gone.

Q: And that also was the end of your career as a Marine flier.

Mr. Darden: Yes. I was sent to London. I was in London when peace came. I will never forget it. We had as a hospital a private home that was used as a naval station. It was in Hyde Park on Rotten Row. People used to ride there occasionally, a few people who had horses. We would go up on the top of the house. It was a lovely home, a big home. We'd walk around on the flat roof. We went up one morning and heard intense antiaircraft fire; antiaircraft guns were all around London as we had heard several times before. Then we noticed there were no bursts in the sky, no explosions in the air, and we knew then that the war was over. Of course, we had been expecting it, there had been rumors. There had been the false armistice. But when we looked up and saw this, we knew this was it. It was an unbelievable thing. We all decamped and went downtown and joined in the celebration. I never saw such an outpouring of people in my life, such enthusiasm. The British were fearfully weary and worn, but they turned out in great numbers. They came from the counties to celebrate. I later came on home. I was home for Christmas in 1918, and I went back and was in and out of the hospital for about a year. I was retired in August 1919. I entered the Columbia Law School in September 1919, and that concluded my journey to the war.

Q: And you began an entirely different career.

Mr. Darden: Entirely different.

Q: And a very illustrious one too.

Mr. Darden: I don't know about that, but it has been a tremendously interesting one.

Darden #2 - 37

Interview Number 2 with the Honorable Colgate W. Darden, Jr.

Place: Army and Navy Club, Washington, D.C.

Date: 20 October 1969

Subject: Naval Legislation

Interviewer: John T. Mason, Jr.

Q: Governor Darden, it's certainly a pleasure to see you again today. This is to be an interview covering your period of service on the Naval Affairs Committee in the House of Representatives. It takes us back to the decade of the 1930s. Governor, tell me about your election to Congress. You came in with the new President.

Mr. Darden: I did. I came in with Mr. Roosevelt, and in truth it was how I came in. I think had there not been a sizable Democratic sweep--my district was largely dependent on federal expenditures because of the great naval operations there--I would not have been elected. There was another reason that cast some doubt on the outcome.

My predecessor was an enormously popular and capable person, Menalcus Lankford.* He was a Republican but had a Democratic family. He comes from a long line of Democrats, but had for reasons of his own embraced the Republican Party as a young man. He had great drawing power from amongst the Democrats and the Republicans alike. He also

---
*Representative Menalcus Lankford (Republican - Virginia).

had a tremendous number of personal friends, and he deserved them. He was a splendid person.

I think my election was due, more than anything else, to the fact that there was a growing sense of change in the country. The Democratic Party was going to win, and that Mr. Roosevelt was going to be President. Probably it was wise to shift over and have a Representative in line with the national party—a person in line for the national party representing us in Washington.

Q: And so you came in, and you were assigned at once to the Naval Affairs Committee.

Mr. Darden: I was most anxious to secure membership on the Naval Affairs Committee, because it meant a great deal to my district and of course, politically to me. I was helped tremendously by Howard Smith, who was already in the House of Representatives; who in turn secured the support of Fred Vinson, who as chairman was an awfully powerful person on the Ways and Means [Committee].* Ways and Means elected members of the committees in the Congress. My whole service in the House of Representatives was on that Naval Affairs Committee.

I was on the committee my first two terms. Then I was defeated. Then I came back to the Congress and was successful in getting on the Naval Affairs Committee again. I served until I resigned to run for

---

*Representative Howard W. Smith (Democrat - Virginia); Representative Frederick M. Vinson (Democrat - Kentucky).

Governor of Virginia in 1941.

Q: You came back in 1939, a hiatus of two years. When you came to the Naval Affairs Committee, of course, the Navy was somewhat in the doldrums, was it not? Economy was the watchword of the time.

Mr. Darden: It was very much in the doldrums, for two reasons. One—economy was the watchword of the time; but also there was a deep feeling held by millions of people in the United States that the naval conferences, the disarmament conference, had opened a new era. That we were in truth moving from an age of war into an age of negotiation for the settlement of world problems. And that the maintenance of a tremendous naval establishment, even a respectable naval establishment, would no longer be necessary. Those two things combined to limit severely the funds available for naval construction.

Q: Did the ranking naval officers have this attitude also?

Mr. Darden: No, they did not. They were very skeptical of it, but they were quite careful in the position they took on the issue in the country. They distrusted it deeply. They sensed the popular feeling in the country and also the commitment of the administration to economy.

It's hard to believe now, but we had come in on a program enunciated by Mr. Roosevelt, that Mr. Hoover was quite extravagant and that federal expenditures should be cut severely, could be cut severely, and would be cut severely.* That proved to be a fearful mistake.

Q: That was an attitude which prevailed perhaps for the first hundred days.

Mr. Darden: That was. I was going to say, I think that marked the first hundred days. Then there was a turnaround, and Mr. Roosevelt moved over carrying a great deal of the Congress with him to an era of free spending.

Q: Induced by the Depression.

Mr. Darden: Yes, an advocate of heavy spending. It was brought on by the Depression, but actually the heavy spending did not solve the economic woes of the country.

When the Second World War came on, we still had this fearful number of unemployed in the nation. The relief programs and other programs had helped, in that they had been a barrier between the people in extreme need and want. But they had not opened up the avenues for employment that we had hoped for.

Consequently, that approach would have had to have been changed,

---
*Franklin D. Roosevelt defeated Herbert C. Hoover in the presidential election of 1932.

Darden #2 - 41

had the war not come. The coming of the war altered the whole thing. It threw us in the other direction and unleashed this gigantic spending program that war always entails.

Q: This idea of spending ourselves out of the Depression had not been tried heretofore, had it, on such a scale?

Mr. Darden: No, I believe not. We tried it on a sizable scale but nothing like the scale we know today in dealing with current difficulties. We tried in public works programs, and other things, and we also engaged in the limitation of production, the slaughtering of pigs. It seems now awful foolish as you look back on it--getting rid of surpluses by destroying them when there were thousands of hungry people in the United States that needed them. To say nothing about people in other parts of the world.

Q: At the inception of the Roosevelt Administration and its program I discovered proposals of various kinds that the budget of the Navy be cut by 5% or so, that civilians in the Navy Department be dismissed, at least 10% of them. The Secretary of the Navy was quoted as saying he thought the Navy could spare 700 officers and 2,000 men without any great difficulty--all of this. Did the committee have any action to take in such matters, or was this an administrative thing?

Mr. Darden: It was largely administrative. One thing we did points out the extreme situation that existed. We recommended legislation to the Congress, and they passed it, giving an academic degree to the graduates of Annapolis. I think the military committee did the same thing for West Point, although I don't recollect for sure on that. Having graduated the Annapolis boys, we did not commission them but turned them off into civil life.

Q: There were no billets for the men.

Mr. Darden: No billets; they could not go to the fleet or to the naval shore stations. There again, two things prompted that. One---economy, two---the belief that the great armament days were over and that we were moving into a new era of human affairs.

Q: Simultaneously, were your appointments to the Naval Academy cut down in number?

Mr. Darden: I don't remember, but I assume that they were. I expect they must have been. My recollection on that is not clear.

The naval yards were greatly reduced. I remember that employment at the naval yard in Portsmouth, Virginia---which was part of my congressional district, the Second Congressional District, and is still a part of the Second Congressional District, although the counties and substantial areas elsewhere have been taken out of it and put in other districts---had fallen drastically and was kept low. The work alloted to the yard was very limited.

Q: Before we began to tape you said another factor in this whole picture at the time was a real concern that Japan might be offended by...

Mr. Darden: It was a very interesting thing. There was running through the government, not to the extent that I saw it later on, a feeling that everything should be done by the United States to ensure the people of Japan of our good will and our desire to get along with them.

It's particularly interesting, because Japan was already moving into Asia then. Its earlier attacks in China and Manchuria had already taken place. They had sizable land armies there operating. They were engaged in what appeared to be, at least, a very aggressive course in Asia.

That had no effect on the United States, at least as far as I remember. It was thought, notwithstanding all of that, it was very important that we not provoke them in any way. Later on, it got to be very acute, and we adopted a lot of subterfuge.

We wanted to fortify, to clear out the harbor at Guam in the late Thirties, so that it would be readily usable for submarines and larger naval ships. There were a great many coral heads in the harbor at Guam that needed to be gotten out, and other work would be done.

We had a bill before our committee that became known as the Guam

Darden #2 - 44

Fortification Bill. It brought down on us hordes of people who said that we were just provoking Japan and that nobody needed Guam, that the legislation was nonsense and ought not to pass. Finally, the bill was withdrawn, and the thing was stuck around in the Public Works Bill somewhere; and the work was done.

Q: It was accomplished anyway?

Mr. Darden: It was accomplished, but it was a deceptive operation on the part of the government. I think that Congress would have passed the legislation, if we had gotten it out and presented it. The consideration of it had created quite a stir. I remember the people who appeared before our committee. They were very earnest people; they were not what we often call crackpots. These people simply believed that any fortification, any work in the Pacific indicated an enlargement of naval power, and that work in the Pacific was in error and we should avoid it. As a concession to them, the legislation was withdrawn by the department from our committee. Later on, the work was done in another way.

Q: Governor, this question of Guam and its fortification also became a policy position of the Republican Party in the Congress, did it not? They were opposed to it.

Mr. Darden: I think they were. It is the late Thirties we're talking about; we were moving on toward war then. I think it likely the Republicans opposed us, because it afforded an excellent opportunity to embarrass us, the Democrats.

They opposed on the ground that we were getting ready to plunge the country into war---and consequently should be distrusted.

Q: Were we totally unaware of Japanese activities in the Caroline and Gilbert Islands which were near to...

Mr. Darden: No, I think not. I think there was a fair knowledge of their operations there. If for no other reason, that they had closed off the area from the rest of the world. They wouldn't allow anybody in there. It was not difficult to deduce from that that what they were doing there was not particularly in the interest of world peace. I think that there was a fairly sound estimate by our naval people of what was going on there. In truth, I expect they overestimated it rather than underestimated it, because they were denied access to that area.

Q: Certainly the Navy---its studies and its war games, the drawing up of war games at the Naval War College and so forth---always in those years thought of the enemy in terms of Japan.

Mr. Darden: I imagine so.

Darden #2 - 46

Q: So there was a kind of dichotomy between Navy thinking...

Mr. Darden: There was a sharp dichotomy, no doubt about that. I expect that is always true to a degree. Your armed services are very much more inclined to guess that there will be a resort to force than your civil population until the thing reaches fever heat. Then the civil population jumps ahead of the military thinking and is willing to give them commitments beyond their capacity, the civilians not having prepared them for it.

Q: When these proposals were made for reduction of personnel and reduction in the amount of money budgeted for the Navy, I believe that Chairman Vinson was opposed to these moves.*

Mr. Darden: I would guess so. My recollection is not clear on that, but I do not believe he actively opposed them. He had the hearings before the committee, and the committee went along. That committee was absolutely dominated by the chairman. I've known many committees in the House of Representatives, but I've never known one that was as completely run by the chairman as the Navy Committee. And yet it was harmonious and a very happy situation. We all got along very well together. We thought alike to a considerable degree. We were interested in supporting the Navy as much as we could. The Navy was very good in its public relations back in those days, with the Congress.

---
*Representative Carl Vinson (Democrat - Georgia).

Darden #2 - 47

Q: Was it indeed? Talk about that.

Mr. Darden: Excellent, it was excellent. I don't know, I won't say that it is not good now; I simply don't know.

Q: The reason I say "do elaborate on that" is because the Navy from time to time has been credited with not really having much know-how, in terms of public relations—certainly during the war.

Mr. Darden: It was, in those days, superb really. They had a fine group of officers at headquarters here that were very accommodating to the committee. They were very willing to explain what they were trying to do and why they were trying to do it. They were good witnesses and frank and open witnesses. Nothing that I have learned since the days of the committee leads me to believe that they at any time misled us. The only misleading thing that I look back on—this came not from the naval officers, I think the information they gave us they absolutely believed—they insisted that Hitler's submarine force was very much greater than it was. After the collapse of the Germans, the Third Reich, when the records could be seen, the writers found that Hitler had quite a limited submarine force. More especially when you consider that a certain percentage of them had to be imported all the time for repairs, in rotation. That's the only serious miscalculation that I remember the Navy ever making. That, I'm confident, was not made wittingly or intentionally to frighten us into appropriations, as the military forces are often accused of, but rather because the information given over to the Navy indicated a greater undersea strength than that which actually existed.

Q: The intelligence on which their reports were based.

Mr. Darden: It might be that part of it was due to the intelligence being fed outside by the Germans themselves. There at a time...

Q: That's not an unknown technique.

Mr. Darden: Not an unknown technique, by any means. I saw another example of it right at the last, in desperate days. In the spring of '41, I think it was, before I left the Congress, the Germans sent to Washington a film showing their advance through Europe. It was taken up and shown confidentially to us in the Congress, the military committees and the naval committees, and as far as I can remember to the other members who wanted to come to see it.

It was a terrifying thing. It showed the effectiveness of the German land power, the destructive power of the German planes—their dive-bombers—and their motorized and mechanized forces and how rapidly they moved. They were moving heavy artillery and the infantry more rapidly than you could move cavalry back in my day during the First World War. They showed us pictures of sweeping down through Belgium, through these Belgian villages, setting up of machine guns.

Darden #2 - 49

It was a sound track thing, you could hear the rattle of the machine gun bullets on the houses and streets as they fired down the street.

I'm satisfied that the picture was furnished the United States and shown us with an idea of convincing us that the situation was hopeless abroad and that nothing could be done.

Q: It was a juggernaut that...

Mr. Darden: That nobody could stop, that the war was lost, and that nobody could do anything about it.

In the same way, it might well have been true that the submarine strength was being furnished us by people who were bent on impressing us with their invincibility at sea. But I don't know. I do know of my own reading since that the calculations given the Naval Committee and the fleet submarine strength as it was developed by researchers after the war were vastly different. The German fleet was nothing like as strong underwater as we were told that it was.

Q: Sir, who were some of these representatives from the Navy who made such good presentations before your committee?

Mr. Darden: There were any number of them---Admiral Standley, who was the Chief of Naval Operations, Admiral Nimitz, Admiral Land, Admiral

King, and many others.*

Q: Admiral Leahy, was he?**

Mr. Darden: Leahy was awfully good, and awfully effective as a witness. Admiral Stark, who was a perfectly fine naval officer, who was done a great injustice by this government after the Pearl Harbor thing.*** He was made, in part, a scapegoat there. It was entered on his record, I think. I understand from people in the Navy that it has since been removed. He was not to be given important sea commands after that. He was later sent to London. He was a fine naval officer, he's still living, a fine person. What the United States did there, it did to its eternal shame. There was no excuse in the world for the mistreatment of that officer by the President and the government.

There was Cook, who was head of Aeronautics.**** There were younger officers. There was Rawlings, a Virginian who retired some

---

*Admiral William H. Standley, USN, Chief of Naval Operations from 1933 to 1937. Rear Admiral Chester W. Nimitz, USN, was Chief of the Bureau of Navigation prior to World War II. Rear Admiral Emory S. Land, USN, Chief of the Bureau of Construction and Repair, 1932-1937. Admiral Ernest J. King, USN, who was Chief of the Bureau of Aeronautics, 1933-1936, and Chief of Naval Operations, 1942-1945.
**Admiral William D. Leahy, USN, Chief of Naval Operations from 1937 to 1939.
***Admiral Harold R. Stark, USN, Chief of Naval Operations from 1939 to 1942.
****Rear Admiral Arthur B. Cook, USN, Chief of the Bureau of Aeronautics from 1936 to 1939.

years back as an admiral.* There was Admiral Bowen.** Admiral Smith, who later became president of University of South Carolina.*** There are just no end of them.

The strong point, the great thing was, at least in my opinion, that never did the Naval Committee feel that they were misleading them in any way. If they did feel it, no member of the committee ever gave expression to that within my hearing. I never heard one of them accuse the Navy of indirection, or of not being entirely frank and candid with us. Certainly insofar as those days were concerned, I think that the relations between the Congress, the Naval Committee, and the Navy could not have been better.

One of the kingpins in that was Carl Vinson, who was awful close to them. He used to have a great hand in running the Navy. They'd come up to his office and sit around and talk about the legislation. They got along very well.

There later was an estrangement, but that was after I left the Congress. I think they made that up before Carl left the Congress, but there were a few years in there. When you talk to him, you might find out more about it.

---

*Norborne L. Rawlings, a member of the Construction Corps. As a lieutenant commander in the 1930s he was stationed at the Norfolk Navy Yard in Darden's district. He eventually retired as a rear admiral in 1947.
  **Rear Admiral Harold G. Bowen, USN, Chief of the Bureau of Engineering from 1935 to 1939.
  ***Rear Admiral Norman M. Smith, USN, Chief of the Bureau of Yards and Docks from 1933 to 1937.

Q: They were trusting him in this period very much.

Mr. Darden: Absolutely, and he trusted them. In later years, something intervened there that pulled them apart. He was their stoutest friend. He ran the committee just like he ran his own house out here at Chevy Chase.

We were all very fond of him. We were inclined to do whatever he said in the end had to be done, or had better be done, or what he wanted done.

We didn't suit the Republicans all the time, but by and large we got along with them pretty good, because they were interested in a competent, good naval force. They didn't make it a party issue. They were not willing to weaken the Navy, at least I didn't think they were. Of course, one of the outstanding fellows over on the Republican side was Mel Maas, who was a reserve officer in the Marine Corps.* He was a great military man. He was always right in there with Vinson, supporting the Navy and helping them in any way he could.

Q: Was Fred Britten still on the Committee?**

Mr. Darden: Fred Britten was on, but went off. He, again, was a very stout Navy man. He was from Chicago, wasn't he?

---

*Representative Melvin J. Maas (Republican - Minnesota).
**Representative Fred A. Britten (Republican - Illinois).

Darden #2 - 53

Q: Yes.

Mr. Darden: Fred Britten went off in my second term, as I remember it.

Q: He had been chairman for a brief period some time or other.

Mr. Darden: Yes. He was a very nice person, very attractive person. He was very considerate of those of us who were young members coming on. Of course, in the Thirties there were a lot of new people up here, a great many.

Q: Sir, there were some specific questions which came before your committee. Perhaps you could comment on some of them. There was a question raised, I believe, about the advisability of establishing a base for the whole fleet at San Pedro, California. This was a controversial thing, I guess.

Mr. Darden: I don't believe it ever reached the point where in the committee it was regarded as a big issue. If it did, I don't remember it.

Q: What about the question of lighter than air craft and the future of Lakehurst as a base for dirigibles?

Darden #2 - 54

Mr. Darden: Lighter than air craft was given a lot of attention and thought by the committee. There was a great deal of support for it, for the naval officer that ran it and very successfully. Was it Rosendahl?*

Q: Rosendahl.

Mr. Darden: It always had a friendly hearing on the Committee. It was not pursued because I think they thought, and the Navy finally came to the same conclusion, that it was not the way the Navy should go. That it was heavier than air.

Q: Of course, there had been that disaster with the Akron.** I believe that members of the Naval Affairs Committee plus members of other committees, maybe a committee from the Senate, had investigated this disaster.

Mr. Darden: I believe so. My recollection on that is not sharp enough to tell you.

Q: There was another very minor issue, I suppose, but rather amusing. At the outset of your term, when it was apparent that prohibition was

---

*Commander Charles E. Rosendahl, USN.
**The rigid airship USS Akron (ZRS-4) was lost at sea during a storm in April 1933 with a heavy loss of life.

going to be repealed. There was some question about the Navy and liquor on naval bases and naval ships.

Mr. Darden: That was an earlier issue. Liquor was taken off naval ships by Mr. Daniels, when he was Secretary of the Navy.*

Q: Yes, I know. But with the repeal of the Constitutional amendment and the return of liquor...**

Mr. Darden: Yes, I believe there was some discussion as to whether or not they should go back to the old Navy days of permitting a ration. I don't believe there was ever any great support for that. There might have been a good deal of laughing and talking about it, but I don't believe it ever had much of a political basis.

Q: I see. There was another very minor issue which involved labor. That was the use of Navy bands on radio and so forth.

Mr. Darden: I think that's always an issue from time to time. It's been for a long time. You mean the Musicians' Union—complaining about the use of the naval band and cutting union members out of

---

*Josephus Daniels, Secretary of the Navy from 1913 to 1921, revoked liquor mess for officers in July 1914.
**The Eighteenth Amendment prohibiting the manufacture, sale, or transportation of intoxicating liquors, passed in 1919, was repealed by the Twenty-first Amendment in 1933.

employment. I believe it's something that's just had to be resolved year to year. I don't believe it's ever been fully and finally settled. I expect to see it erupt again from time to time. It's erupted many times in the past.

Q: One interesting point which the administration seemed to make must have been emphasized in the committee also, in terms of the shipbuilding program that was in being in '33, '34. The emphasis was on the number of jobs it would provide.

Mr. Darden: Yes, that was always, as it is today, a selling point in any naval program. It should not be the primary one by any means, although it is in certain areas. The primary one is the defense of the United States, or the Navy as an arm of foreign policy.

There's a great deal of employment bound up in a ship construction program, not just the building of the ship itself—the preparation of steel in remote places, and the electrical systems. And now it's unbelievably sophisticated, costly, and intricate. They employ thousands of people far removed from the assembly area the atomic engines are made.

I think the Enterprise's engines were made by Westinghouse, weren't they? That's my recollection. I know we built the Enterprise at Newport News some years back.*

---

*The USS Enterprise (CVAN-65), the Navy's first nuclear-powered aircraft carrier, was built by Newport News Shipbuilding and Dry Dock Company and commissioned in November 1961. Her steam turbines were indeed supplied by Westinghouse, as Darden remembered.

Employment has always played a very large part in naval appropriations. It's a specialized works program.

Q: In those early days of your service on Naval Affairs, Claude Swanson from your own state of Virginia was Secretary, and Mr. Roosevelt named Henry Latrobe Roosevelt as Assistant Secretary of the Navy. Did they also appear before the committee, and how effective were they?*

Mr. Darden: Mr. Swanson, to my recollection, never came before the committee. He'd had a stroke, and he was not well; he was quite frail. I knew him fairly well, and I used to go in to see him down at the Navy Department.

Occasionally, Mr. Roosevelt came. He was a very effective Assistant Secretary. He carried the load of the department. He was very close to Mr. Swanson; they were very friendly. He would come occasionally and testify.

Most of the testimony was done by the naval officers themselves. A good deal of the department work was done by Arch Oden, who was Mr. Swanson's old secretary when he was in the Senate.** He moved him down to the Navy Department when he went down there. A lot of our business, and my business I attended to with Arch.

---

*Claude A. Swanson, Secretary of the Navy from 1933 to 1939; Henry L. Roosevelt, Assistant Secretary of the Navy from 1933 to 1936.
**Archibald Oden.

Q: In 1934, as I perused a review of affairs pertaining to the Navy, I noticed a difference in the Roosevelt budget of that year. There was much greater generosity toward the Navy, and there was a provision for many new ships. There was also a partial restoration of pay cuts. Would you comment on this change? There seems to have been a watershed there somewhere.

Mr. Darden: There was a watershed. That marked the turn in Mr. Roosevelt's philosophy. He was moving from the extreme position of the year before, the economy's position, over to a spending position. It was not hard for him to do in the Navy, because the Navy had always had a preferred place with him. He'd been Assistant Secretary.* He liked very much to ride around on the big ships, and be at naval stations, and take his salute and carry on in that fashion.

Q: As a matter of fact, he reviewed the fleet.

Mr. Darden: Up in New York, the Naval Committee went up there. It was just exactly what he liked, that was the kind of thing he was engaged in. I think he was on the Indianapolis. They were passing in review, he was taking the salute, carrying on at a great rate.**

---

*Franklin D. Roosevelt was Assistant Secretary of the Navy from 1913 to 1920, during the administration of President Woodrow Wilson.
**President Roosevelt presided over a fleet review in New York Harbor aboard the cruiser USS Indianapolis (CA-35) on 31 May 1934.

He loved it, he loved the pageantry, he liked everything about the Navy. Given half a chance, he was perfectly willing to move over and help us.

Now, the public sentiment in the country was such that he didn't do it directly with the naval appropriations bill. He put some money in the public works bill and turned it over to Harold Ickes to administer.* He was a crusty old fellow.

Q: That was the only way he could get those funds.

Mr. Darden: The only way he could get them, yes. He turned them over to Harold Ickes. My guess is that he told Harold Ickes that he was willing for us to have funds—the various yards. Ickes let the money out on that basis. Harold Ickes handled it. He didn't appear to know the slightest thing about the Navy. Harold Ickes did not, I think, know one end of a ship from another.

We'd have to go and sit with him and talk about our needs. It was a preposterous operation, but it served to get a good deal of new construction under way, and to keep going.

Then there was the setting in motion of spending. There was the restoration of some of the cuts, and bringing back a few of the Annapolis classes and letting them come back into the Navy, as I remember it. But not so many; I think they came back in larger numbers later on. The last came back in the Second World War.

---

*Harold L. Ickes, Secretary of the Interior from 1933 to 1945.

Darden #2 - 60

Q: In connection with that upturn in the fortunes in the Navy in that year '34, there were two interesting bills before your committee, one of which was adopted. One by Fred Britten proposed that 101 ships be built in a program which would extend through 1938, I believe. The one which was adopted was by Carl Vinson, which proposed 102, one more than the other. The reason was, to bring our Navy up to the parity.

Mr. Darden: Not to abandon the treaties, but reach treaty parity.

Q: Up to that point, we hadn't been concerned with bringing it up.

Mr. Darden: No, we had not. There again, that was done in order to give the world double assurance of our desire for peace. Not only did we join in the naval limitation, but we did not then build the fleet to the limit. We junked some of the ships that were under construction. Some of them we switched over to other types. I think the first carriers came out of the battle cruiser program, as it was switched over to carriers. We did not build to our limits. We wished to say to the world, and to say to our own people---those who believed that building of armaments incited war---that our actions gave absolute assurance that what we wanted was peace.

As the Thirties went on, that sentiment was changing, because we were arriving at the opinion that we were not as secure as we might be. There was growing trouble in Asia, and there was then the rise of Hitler in Germany, which was alarming. Hitler came in to power in '33 when he became Chancellor.* He set out on a course which was disturbing to the rest of the world. That was reflected in the armament expenditure here as the Thirties dragged along.

Q: What was the attitude of the British toward their navy at that time? Were they up to treaty strength?

Mr. Darden: I think not. I think there the financial distress was even greater than our own.

Q: One aspect of the Vinson bill which I hope you'll comment on, is the provision for over 1,100 planes for the Navy. Would this indicate a growing interest in naval aviation?

Mr. Darden: It indicates and was in truth not only a growing interest in it, but a growing conviction that the plane was a weapon of great power. And that we would have to move on in the development of it. Carl was very forward-looking in those things. That was one of the reasons he was so popular with the Navy. He moved them along into these new fields, and helped them secure the money in the Congress to pay for them. He was a great carrier man, and a great aircraft man.

That was evidence of the coming into its own of naval power. Naval aviation, in my very early days, and the days we were talking about when we were here before, was at best a small, feeble effort.

---

*Adolf Hitler, Chancellor of Germany from 1933 to 1945.

In the Thirties, it had reached substantial proportions.

Q: The next phase was the shoring up of shore stations, and appropriating money for this purpose. Do you recall anything in that area?

Mr. Darden: I do, it was a little more than shoring up. It was the development of a large number of new stations for the training of aviators and others. The Hepburn Report, if you remember it...*

Q: That was in '37.

Mr. Darden: Yes. It was a marked enlargement.

Going back to '34, the old naval stations under the general economies that had been forced on them were in a pretty weak situation. We began in '34 to improve them and to put in better machinery, more modern machinery for the repair of ships and things of that kind.

I think there was, in '34 and '35, a growing realization that you couldn't turn loose power as much as you might want to do it; that it was dangerous to let it slide from your hand; and that the universal peace would not follow upon a withering away of the armed forces. That properly, the armed forces would wither away after the coming of

---

*The Hepburn Board, formed by President Roosevelt in 1938 and headed by Admiral Arthur J. Hepburn, USN, was tasked with making recommendations for the improvement of naval facilities.

universal peace. Do I make myself clear?

Q: Yes, indeed you do. Men were becoming a little more realistic about world affairs.

Mr. Darden: And maybe a little more cynical about it, and more apprehensive. Maybe cynical is too sharp a word, too hard a word. They saw on all sides a world which seemed to be moving towards force again. The Asia thing was bad, the European situation was very bad.

Q: And yet, you had in the Congress, still plenty of men who fought the development of this idea. In 1936, I believe it was, the naval appropriation was something over $500 million, which was an unprecedented amount. It met with a great deal of opposition from men like Vito Marcantonio and Gerald Nye.*

Mr. Darden: Yes. Vito Marcantonio was an interesting person. He was active in the House of Representatives then. He bitterly opposed the program of arming the United States. He opposed it until--this is probably a harsh charge, but I think the record will bear me out in it--the German-Russian quarrel. Then he was willing to throw his weight toward an army on the Russian axis. He was very partial to the Soviets, in his thinking and in his general attitude in the House. Up

---
*Representative Vito Marcantonio (American Labor - New York); Senator Gerald P. Nye (Republican - North Dakota).

until that time, he'd been an implacable foe of rearming the United States.

Q: That was the time when you had the munitions hearings.

Mr. Darden: No, that was some little time after that. That was two or three years after that; the munitions hearings were around '35 or '36. The stout position taken by Marcantonio came after the outbreak of war, which was '39. There was sharp opposition in the Thirties to building up our armed forces. It was thought by many that an armament industry was unnecessary in the United States, and that the maintenance of strong armed forces was sheer waste. If only we held out the hand of friendship to the rest of the world, that we could settle our problems at a conference table. Nobody needed a navy, nor did they need an army. If you go back and read the Congressional Record of that time, you'll be surprised by the people who subscribed to it. Many of them are now dead, but some are still living.

Q: And this was an honest opinion.

Mr. Darden: Yes, it was, by and large. There are one or two exceptions, I think. By and large, they were groups of people, just as the witnesses who appeared before our committee, of interested civilians who believed that it was all a mistake. Jeannette Rankin was one, and there was no question about Miss Rankin's deep conviction on the thing.* There's never been the slightest doubt in my mind.

Q: And she was back in the Congress again?

Mr. Darden: She was back in the Congress and voted against war in the First World War. In my time when she was back in, her views had not changed. As a matter of fact, she had far more friends and supporters of her views about the First World War then, because so many people had become disillusioned with Europe and our whole commitment there. I never had any doubt about her dedication and belief that we could have world peace if only we'd take the lead and disarm the United States.

Q: In that same vein, in 1937 Ev Dirksen had a bill which I believe came before your committee---to restrain the Navy from maneuvers and war games beyond the 300-mile limit.**

Mr. Darden: That, of course, was part and parcel of the sentiment of not offending Japan in any way. I don't remember his bill, but I do remember he was very dubious about our activities. He was then in the House. He was a very capable member of the House; he left it because of the failure of his eyes when he thought he was going blind. I

---
*Representative Jeannette Rankin (Republican - Montana). She was the only member of Congress to vote against declaration of war after the Japanese attacked Pearl Harbor in December 1941.
**Representative Everett M. Dirksen (Republican - Illinois).

remember sitting in the House the day that he got up and made the statement that he was going to have to give up because he was losing his sight. He was popular and he had the sympathy of the whole House. He carried on a very courageous campaign and got his sight back. They got him back over in the Senate.

That was part of not having the fleet maneuver too far out in the Pacific, because it might offend Japan. Do not do this, and do not do that, lest it offend Japan. Japan was then up to her neck in Asia, in aggression in Manchuria.

Q: In retrospect, it seems like a rather timid position.

Mr. Darden: It was a timid position, and I think so regarded by the Japanese war establishment and by the Japanese Manchurian army. I've been told, and I expect this is true, that had the Japanese Navy had the upper hand, the Japanese would not have entered the war as they did. The influence of the generals, especially those of the Asiatic Army---which was a crackerjack army---swept the Japanese people on to war with us. Those people knew nothing of the military power of the United States. Their whole military life had been spent on the Asian mainland, or in Japan. The navy knew; they'd been over there. They had seen some of our ships and stations. But more than that, they knew something of the industrial power of the United States, which is so determining in war. I've heard people in whom I have confidence say that had the naval officers been in ascendance there---if there had been an admiral instead of Tojo there advising them—that it's likely that the assault that was made on Pearl Harbor would never have been made.* Although, the Navy delivered the blow after the decision was taken, and did it very ably. The taking of it, they thought, was a decision by other people who were less well advised as to the formidable position of the United States.

Q: Sir, you were a member of this Board of Visitors for the Naval Academy. Was this in the early part of the Thirties?

Mr. Darden: I was on that board two or three times, I recollect. As I remember, they would select members from the Naval Committee, and Carl would put me on that and send me over along with others. I remember a very interesting thing about that service.

We were always struggling to enlarge the liberal arts training at the Naval Academy and to lighten up somewhat on its commitment to science, mathematics, and those things of naval instruction.

Q: On what theory?

Mr. Darden: On the theory that a general education was of extreme value to a naval officer and that he'd be, in the long run, a much better naval officer if he was given a broad liberal education.

---

*Lieutenant General Hideki Tojo, Japanese Army, served as Minister of War and Prime Minister in the early 1940s.

Q: And the technical knowledge would come with graduate work?

Mr. Darden: Yes. I'm not at all certain but that the education, the liberal education of the universities and colleges would not be better for young men training to be naval officers, leaving the naval work itself entirely to the graduate field. The service academies would then become graduate institutions. There is this caveat. That is that they cannot be indoctrinated with discipline and naval life so well when they reach the graduate age. Young men, just starting in college, can be most molded in the Navy's tradition. That's what the Navy wanted then. I'm not in touch with it now. They argued, and I think with considerable force, that graduate life was too late for them.

At any rate, we struggled with having more work in liberal arts. We never accomplished a good deal, because the naval program was terribly crowded. You had the drilling and discipline and other things thrown in, and the naval sciences. There wasn't but so much time left for English, history, philosophy and such things.

It was always a pleasant assignment. I remember old Senator Walsh from Massachusetts---he was on it once or twice---and other members back in those days.*

Q: When you returned to the Congress in '39, all sorts of things were

---

*Senator David I. Walsh (Democrat - Massachusetts), chairman of the Senate Naval Affairs Committee.

happening in the defense area. We'd had the Neutrality Acts, one of '35, and the renewal in '37. In '39, you had the beginning of the implementation of the Hepburn Report.

Mr. Darden: Yes. You also had still a sizable sentiment in Congress that this problem abroad was not really a problem, and that we'd better mind our own business and be very careful that we did not get involved.

Q: How long did that continue?

Mr. Darden: It continued right up until Pearl Harbor really.

Q: Didn't Poland have something to do with a change?*

Mr. Darden: It had something to do with the change, but there was a strong body of opinion. My guess is that even after Poland and the German drive to the east, without Japan and without Pearl Harbor, nobody could have gotten a declaration of war through the Congress. I think the sentiment within the United States was overwhelmingly in favor of staying out of Europe. Maybe not overwhelmingly, but substantially in favor of, would be a better word.

---

*Poland was invaded by Nazi Germany and the Soviet Union in September 1939, less than a month after these two countries entered a non-aggression pact with each other.

Q: But did you not have all sorts of infringements on a strict neutral position in terms of the destroyer deal, the bases, and all the rest?

Mr. Darden: Yes, we did. We had another thing that the Congress did not then know about. Roosevelt was working on his own hook; he was using the fleet in the Atlantic in a guarding operation and a fighting operation.

Q: He called it neutrality patrol.

Mr. Darden: Yes, but the Congress couldn't find out much about it. He wouldn't let out much information about it. The Navy was very guarded; they told us a little something about it. They were mighty cautious in their talking, because they didn't know what would happen to them. Mr. Roosevelt was committed to support for England.

The destroyer deal, which was, I believe, one of his ideas, was a very good deal really.* It resulted in giving to the British help. There ran through all of that, however, an utter unreality actually—namely that with some material help, Hitler could be stopped.

I don't know if you remember—Churchill made so many great speeches—the one in which he said, "Give us the tools, and we'll

---

*In an agreement formally concluded on 2 September 1940, Britain ceded to the United States sovereign rights for 99 years over sites for naval, military, and air bases in the Bahamas, Jamaica, Antigua, St. Lucia, Trinidad, and British Guiana, in exchange for 50 four-stack destroyers built during or shortly after World War I.

finish the job."* It was a thrilling thing, because the people of the United States reacted to it with a feeling that here was a courageous people. And the British were courageous in that year they stood alone. Nobody did more to forge the weapons of victory than Churchill with the stirring speeches that he made. They touched the very heart of the American people.

Q: We still hoped that we could avoid...

Mr. Darden: Not only hoped, but believed we could.

Q: We'd write the checks...

Mr. Darden: We'd write the checks, and they'd do the fighting. We'd send them the supplies, give them the destroyers, and in the end things would come right.

Hitler moved on with the superb war machine of his toward the knocking out of the world. He came powerfully close to doing it. Nobody will ever know how really close he came.

Q: How did the President get away with his solo operation, so to speak?

---

*Sir Winston Churchill, British Prime Minister from 1940 to 1945 and from 1951 to 1955.

Mr. Darden: He got away with it by abhorring war. Do you remember his speech out in Chicago that he despised war, abhorred war?*

Q: The Quarantine Speech?

Mr. Darden: Yes, and talking peace. I never will forget in the last election, he ran on the basis of keeping us out of war. He was already fighting in the Atlantic then. The votes had hardly been counted before we were moving to the final involvement. Mr. Roosevelt knew—was bound to have known, with his knowledge and contacts that he had—that the deteriorating situation abroad required the intervention of the United States if it was to be saved. The French had already collapsed, the British were outnumbered terribly. We had to save them from deep trouble.

The German Army—there was current talk around Washington that the Russian Army wouldn't be able to stop it. I remember the expression which you heard from time to time that "it [the German Army] would go through Russia like a hot knife through butter." That proved to be a miscalculation, which the Germans found out in the end. But that was the belief in high circles here.

The American people in the campaign of the fall, if you go back and read the papers, were assured that they were going to stay out of war. A vote for the Democrats was a vote to keep them out of war.

---

*The President made the speech in October 1937. For details on its effectiveness, see John McVickar Haight, Jr., "FDR's 'Big Stick,'" U.S. Naval Institute Proceedings, July 1980, pages 68-73.

Darden #2 - 73

Q: Is there anything that comes back to you from the Naval Affairs Committee in that period? Those two years.

Mr. Darden: No, not particularly. Other than a sense of the necessity of arming, of building ships, and putting the Navy on a war footing.

Q: Was this easier to accomplish?

Mr. Darden: Yes, but it was impossible a few years before. The Congress wasn't of a mind to build anything. The idea of talking to them about a battleship would be like introducing a snake into things, a poisonous snake. It scared everybody to death.

By '39 and '40, we had moved to a point of extreme urgency and fear that made the task much easier.

Q: In 1940, I have a note on a fight made by Chairman Vinson. It was an amendment to the Selective Service Act or Bill involving conscription of industry. Now we were still at peace. He argued for a rather moderate measure which wouldn't invoke penalties on the manufacturer who didn't attend to the orders.

Mr. Darden: As I remember it, that was a softening of Mr. Baruch's plan.* Mr. Baruch had a plan for conscription of labor and industry, everything, in war. I don't remember clearly Carl's plan. I'm reasonably certain of one thing--if it was his plan, it was one that had been generally agreed on by the administration. Because they worked closely with the chairmen in the House. Carl was very friendly with the President. He used to go down and talk with him about the Navy, one thing and another. He'd known him back in the old days when he was Assistant Secretary. If he had a plan, I would guess that it was a plan that had the blessing of the administration. But I have no recollection of any details of it.

Q: Was there any legislation that pertained to the eventual turning over of the destroyers? Was there anything necessary there?

Mr. Darden: No, I don't believe there was anything other than the ratification of the plan by the Congress. I believe the preparation of them, the fitting of them in the yards was administrative entirely. Mr. Roosevelt went right along with that. He probably had gone along some distance before he got the authorization. I don't mean by that, that he violated a law. He'd been putting the destroyers in shape to where they were usable. Many of them, I think, had been laid up.

Q: They were termed obsolete.

---
*Bernard M. Baruch, Chairman of the War Production Board (WPB) in the 1940s.

Mr. Darden: I think that was rather a political phrase to help along the idea of giving them to the British. I think they were being withdrawn and fitted and gotten in shape, so that when the permission was given, they could quickly be moved over into British service.

The trade of destroyers did give us bases that were valuable. It gave us the Trinidad base and other bases from which we could operate.

Q: And also Newfoundland.

Mr. Darden: Yes. The heart of the thing was to give the English the ships. They had to have them. They didn't have time to build, or means to build, or manpower to build.

Q: That must have been a very exciting time to serve on the committee.

Mr. Darden: It was, it was a tremendous exciting time; and to a degree, frightening. But it's more frightening now than it was then. I suppose it's because those of us who are part of it are old, and we look back on it with greater apprehension. So many things seemed possible then, about which now you'd be very doubtful, because you've seen such catastrophic changes in the world. It was an enormously exciting period, because the great currents that were sweeping around the world were running at full tide.

Q: What was your basic philosophy about rearmament and building up the Navy, and so forth?

Mr. Darden: I've always felt that without armed power a country is at a disadvantage. Even if it wants to be peaceful, it is at a disadvantage without armed forces. Now it's entirely possible that my thinking was colored sizably by the fact that I represented a great military district. But I doubt it, because as the years have gone on and I've been many years out of the House of Representatives, I'm a long way away from that close association, I still entertain that view today. So I would rather think it was not a result of the political interest. It might have started that way. I'm satisfied now that were the United States to disarm, it would fall victim to aggression within a reasonably short time. I think there is no possibility of living in a world of which we are a part today without a strong military establishment. As unpleasant as that may sound, I think it true. I don't believe we can disarm and survive. I think we'd be swept away before we knew what happened to us. The unfortunate thing is that those who believe the other side, would not then have a chance to arm, even if they changed their minds. It would be too late. If the armaments were not in being, we would be swept away and there'd be no chance of arming.

Q: In the Thirties, we still had that option, didn't we?

Darden #2 - 77

Mr. Darden: Yes, we did, but no longer. I would think that we should nurture in the United States a dedication to international justice and peace supported by strong armed force. Without that—a dedication to justice—armed power would not amount to anything. Armed force without the dedication to justice and peace becomes a vehicle for oppression and dictatorship. Certainly no one would wish to see that happen. The good intentions, the best intentions of our people will never be brought to fruition unless they are backed by power that can defend this country in case it needs to be defended.

Q: Thank you very much, sir.

Mr. Darden: I'm delighted at this opportunity at seeing you again and talking with you.

Q: Governor, you just mentioned Admiral Nimitz and his effectiveness when he appeared before the Naval Affairs Committee.* Would you tell me on tape something about him and his techniques, and so forth?

Mr. Darden: He was a giant in the United States naval service. He was quiet, unassuming, enormously capable, and of unimpeachable integrity. He testified often before our Committee. He never left the Committee with the impression that he had not divulged to them all

---

*Rear Admiral Chester W. Nimitz, USN, Chief of the Bureau of Navigation from 1939 to 1941.

that he knew. He never left us under the impression that he knew everything. He was a superb naval officer who had the complete confidence of every single person on the Naval Committee.

I knew him well and worked with him over some years even after I left the Naval Committee. I saw him from time to time. The last time I saw him, as a matter of fact, he and I were pallbearers at Halsey's funeral here in Washington.* We had a little chat about old times. He was then living on the West Coast. I noticed then for the first time, he was slightly bowed. Before that, he'd been as straight as a ramrod. I always thought of him as, not as the last of the vikings, but probably as the most recent of the vikings. He was an inspiring commander. As I said at the beginning, he was a giant in the naval forces of the United States. Deeply loved, deserved to be loved, self-effacing, but tremendously competent.

Q: He really had done his homework when he appeared before the committee.

Mr. Darden: He never failed to do his homework. He knew what he was talking about. You could bet your last dollar on what he told you. You never had to check it. When he told you something, you never had to go back and look it up to see whether Nimitz was right. No matter

---

*Fleet Admiral William F. Halsey, Jr., USN, who died in 1959.

what the case was, you could bet that was what it was. He had the confidence exceeded by no person that I've ever met in public life in Washington, of the people in the Congress. He was so quiet, and kind of unassuming. You would think he was just coming along, and not a top commander in the Navy. Rank never seemed to mean anything to him. His standing came not from rank, but from sheer and towering ability.

Q: I thank you. That's a wonderful statement.

Index to

Series of Taped Interviews

with

the Honorable Colgate W. Darden, Jr.

Aircraft Maintenance
  Performed between naval training flights in 1918, pp. 12, 15.

Airships
  Item of concern for House Naval Affairs Committee in 1930s, pp. 53-54.

Alcohol
  Repeal of Prohibition in 1933 did not affect U.S. Navy, pp. 54-55.

Aviation
  See: Marine Corps Aviation; Naval Aviation.

Churchill, Winston
  British Prime Minister who thrilled audiences with his speeches during World War II, pp. 70-71.

Congress
  See: Naval Affairs Committee.

Cunningham, Alfred A., Major, USMC
  Marine Corps aviator in World War I, pp. 16, 25.

Darden, Colgate W., Jr.
  Enlisted in French Army in 1916 and served in France, where he got bronchial infection, pp. 1-6; sense of idealism about U.S. war effort, pp. 4-6; received naval aviation training in 1917-1918 after return from France, pp. 6-15, 18; transferred to Marine Corps in 1918 and served with aviation contingent in France, pp. 16-30; Darden injured in spectacular aircraft accident in October 1918 and took some months to recover, pp. 30-36; as member of House Naval Affairs Committee in 1930s and early 1940s, pp. 37-79.

Depression
  Effects of in the United States in 1930s, pp. 40-42.

Destroyers
  See: Great Britain.

DH-4
  Fighter-bomber aircraft flown by Marine Corps in World War I, pp. 22-24, 30-32.

Dirksen, Everett M.
  U.S. Representative who resigned his seat because of eye problems, pp. 65-66.

Disarmament
  Effect on U.S. Navy in 1930s, pp. 39, 43-46, 60, 76-77. See also: Isolationism.

Food
   Quality of for U.S. naval aviation students in 1918, pp. 10-11.

Florida
   Naval aviation training at various sites in the state during World War I, pp. 9-15, 18; Marine Corps aviation training during World War I, pp. 16-23, 33-34.

France
   Darden enlisted in French Army in 1916 and served in France, pp. 1-6; Northern Bombing Group of U.S. fliers operated near Calais in 1918, pp. 24-35.

Geiger, Roy S., Major, USMC
   Commander of a Marine Corps squadron in the Northern Bombing Group in France during World War I, pp. 25-26.

Germany
   German Air Force operations over France in 1918, pp. 28-29; U.S. intelligence estimates of German military and naval strength prior to U.S. entry into World War II, pp. 47-49, 72.

Great Britain
   Darden recuperated in London after aircraft accident in 1918, pp. 35-36; President Franklin D. Roosevelt traded old U.S. destroyers to British in 1940, pp. 70-71, 74-75.

Guam
   U.S. attempts to fortify in 1930s, pp. 43-45.

Gunnery
   Aerial gunnery training in Florida during World War I, pp. 20-23.

H-16
   Large Navy flying boat considered hazardous to fly in World War I, pp. 17-18.

House of Representatives
   See: Dirksen, Everett M.; Maas, Melvin J.; Marcantonio, Vito; Naval Affairs Committee; Rankin, Jeannette; Vinson, Carl.

Ickes, Harold L.
   Secretary of Interior whose department helped fund U.S. shipbuilding program in 1930s, p. 59.

Intelligence
   Estimates of German capabilities prior to U.S. entry into World War II, pp. 47-49.

Isolationism
  Attempts to keep the United States from getting involved in the international scene in the 1930s, pp. 63-65, 69-70, 73, 76-77.

Japan
  U.S. attempts to avoid provoking Japan before World War II, even though it was likely enemy, pp. 43-46, 66-67.

JN-4
  Land biplane flown by the Marine Corps in World War I, p. 19.

Lighter-than-air Craft
  See: Airships.

Liquor
  See: Alcohol.

London
  See: Great Britain.

Maas, Melvin J.
  U.S. Representative who strongly supported Navy in the years leading up to World War II, p. 52.

Maintenance
  See: Aircraft maintenance.

Marcantonio, Vito
  U.S. Representative who had isolationist stance until Germany invaded Russia in 1941, pp. 63-64.

Marine Corps Aviation
  Darden transferred to Marine Corps in 1918 for training and then served with Northern Bombing Group in France, pp. 16-35.

Massachusetts Institute of Technology
  Site of naval aviation ground school training during World War I, pp. 7-9.

N-9
  U.S. naval aircraft used for training in 1918, pp. 12-13.

Naval Academy, U.S.
  Some midshipmen graduated but not commissioned because of Depression in 1930s, later recalled, pp. 41-42, 59; Darden as member of board of visitors examining curriculum in 1930s, pp. 67-68.

Naval Affairs Committee, House of Representatives
   Activities of in 1930s and early 1940s, pp. 37-79.

Naval Aviation
   Darden received training at MIT ground school in 1917, pp. 7-9;
   training at various sites in Florida in 1918, pp. 9-15; supported by
   Congress in 1930s, p. 61.

Nimitz, Chester W., Rear Admiral, USN (USNA, 1905)
   Impressive witness when testifying before Congress as Chief of the
   Bureau of Navigation just prior to World War II, pp. 77-79.

Northern Bombing Group
   U.S. Navy-Marine Corps flying contingent in France during World War
   I, pp. 24-35.

Prohibition
   See: Alcohol.

Rankin, Jeannette
   U.S. Representative with deep isolationist sentiments in both World
   Wars, pp. 64-65.

Roosevelt, Franklin D.
   President in 1930s and 1940s, pp. 37-41, 50, 58-59; 70-72, 74.

Roosevelt, Henry L.
   Assessment of as Assistant Secretary of the Navy in the 1930s, p. 57.

Seaplanes
   Used for U.S. naval aviation training in 1918, pp. 12-14, 17-18.

Shipbuilding Program—U.S. Navy
   Size of in 1930s dictated by various considerations, pp. 39, 56-60, 73.

Shore Stations—Naval
   U.S. facilities needed improvements in the 1930s, p. 62.

Stark, Harold R., Admiral, USN (USNA, 1903)
   U.S. Chief of Naval Operations whom Darden feels was done an
   injustice after the attack on Pearl Harbor, p. 50.

Submarines
   U.S. intelligence overestimated capability of German U-boat force
   prior to World War II, pp. 47-48.

Talbot, Ralph, Second Lieutenant, USMCR
   Medal of Honor winner killed in spectacular aircraft accident in
   France in October 1918, pp. 30-33.

Thomas Scout
  U.S. aircraft used in World War I training, p. 19

Training
  Naval aviation instruction in Massachusetts and Florida in 1917-1918, pp. 7-15, 18, 33-34; Marine Corps aviation training in Florida in 1918, pp. 16-23.

Vinson, Carl
  U.S. Representative who headed House Naval Affairs Committee in 1930s and 1940s, pp. 46, 51-52, 60-61, 73-74.

World War I
  Darden enlisted in French Army in 1916 and served in France, pp. 1-6, naval aviation training in United States during war, pp. 7-15; Marine Corps aviation during the war, pp. 16-36.

World War II
  See: Germany; Great Britain; Stark, Harold R.

www.ingramcontent.com/pod-product-compliance
Lightning Source LLC
Chambersburg PA
CBHW080610170426
43209CB00007B/1390